SANTA BARBARA

HIGHLIGHTS & HISTORY

BY JUDY MAGEE DUGAN

Jama books

To my parents.

Acknowledgements

The contributions of knowledge and resources by businesses, organizations and individuals throughout the community have been invaluable in the preparation of this work. I wish to thank all who have given their time and support to this project.
An extra note of appreciation is due to the following groups and individuals who have been especially helpful: Dennis Roeder, Dr. Travis Hudson, Jill Le Van, Miss Julia Brown, Ed & Georgina Morin, the Santa Barbara Chamber of Commerce, Marin Graphics, UCSB Special Collections, Larson-Bateman, Inc., and Surf & Wear.
Many thanks to Walker Tompkins for his advice and years of research which have been most influential in the preparation of the historical text.

My special thanks to the following people whose advice, efforts and encouragement have made this book possible: Maryann Murphy, my husband, Dick, and Dan Poynter.

Copyright © 1979 by Judith Magee Dugan

jb Jama books

First Edition
Printed in the United States of America

P.O. Box 30751
Santa Barbara, CA 93105

Library of Congress Cataloging in Publication Data
Dugan, Judy Magee, 1951-
    Santa Barbara : highlights & history.

    Includes index.
    1. Santa Barbara, Calif.—History. 2. Santa Barbara, Calif.—Description and travel—Guide-books.

    I. Title.
    F869.S45D83   917.94'91   79-2378

                ISBN 0-934130-01-9 Hard cover

                ISBN 0-934130-00-0 Paperback

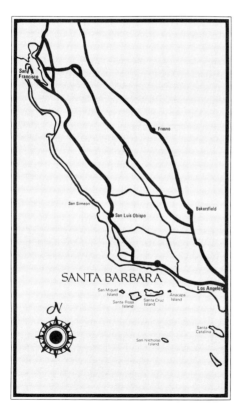

CONTENTS

INTRODUCTION   4

HISTORY   8

HIGHLIGHTS   26

Sunswept palm-lined beaches, harbor sails and a sea of terra-cotta rooftops paint the uncommonly beautiful setting of Santa Barbara. Few places offer as inviting a blend of natural beauty, gentle climate and harmony in man's contributions to the land.

Four cultures, spanning recent centuries, have etched a colorful history along Santa Barbara shores. The Chumash Indians, who followed the more primitive hunting and gathering tribes, may have numbered as many as 12,000 here before their eclipse under Spanish, Mexican and American flags. Each culture has left its imprint on the modern community of Santa Barbara.

Santa Barbara takes her name from a legendary Christian martyr said to have lost her head to her father's sword when he learned she had converted to Christianity. According to legend, the father was instantly struck by a bolt of lightening from a cloudless sky. The young woman has since been considered a protectress against stormy elements, rarely seen in the town that takes her name.

Balmy year-round temperatures generally range in the 60's and 70's, with rains reserved for brief bursts in winter. The unusual East-West coastline plays tricks on those who take bearings from the sun and the sea. The sun traces its path along the coast and in winter can both rise and set over the ocean in a single day. Coupled with the diagonal alignment of streets to both coastal and polar directions, orientation in town can be somewhat challenging. Sweeping city views from El Mirador Clock Tower in the County Courthouse are helpful in understanding the layout of the town.

Since the late 1800's
Santa Barbara's climate and unique
natural features have drawn visitors
and health-seekers from around
the world. Fabulous hotels catered to
wealthy vacationers, many of whom
fell in love with the area and
made it their home. Still attracting
visitors and residents of all ages and
walks of life, Santa Barbara has
pleasures to offer everyone:
sailing, fishing, sun and surf for
beach goers; camping, hiking and
spectacular mountain·views inland;
charming shopping arcades,
art galleries and nearly 80 antique
shops; museums of art, natural
and civic history; botanical and
zoological gardens; theater
and entertainment; restaurants and
nightlife; a colorful summer fiesta in
a parade of annual festivities; several
educational institutions, including
nearby University of California at
Santa Barbara; neighboring attractions
of Danish Solvang and lovely Ojai;
and, for those who enjoy a look at the
past that still enriches the modern
community of Santa Barbara,
her history fills the streets
and is waiting to be explored . . .

A replica of the Chumash plank canoe christened "Helek" (Falcon), was paddled to the Channel Islands by descendants of native Indians. The canoe is now in the halls of the County Courthouse.

HISTORY

THE CHUMASH

For centuries, the Santa Barbara coast was inhabited by peaceful Chumash (Canalino) Indians. They lived from the bounty of sea and land without cultivating the earth. Wild seeds and nuts, seafood and game were eaten instead of domesticated plant and animal life, and fish were ingeniously caught in inland pools by stunning them with the juices of crushed soap plant. Brush huts and scant, if any, clothing met their needs in the gentle climate. Steam huts, similar to modern steambaths, were visited in a daily cleansing ritual and followed by a plunge in cool waters.

Elaborate rock paintings are found in hidden caves and crevices throughout Chumash country and were likely created in rites of magic and spiritualism. Shamans, medicine men considered to have mystical influence with good and evil spirits, are thought to have painted the rock walls, possibly under the hallucinogenic influence of Toloache (Jimson Weed).* Earthen pigments were ground with plant or animal oils and applied with sticks, frayed yucca leaves, or brushes of animal tails. If you drive up Painted Cave Road off San Marcos Pass (154), you may peek through a protective grating at the Indian geometrics in one such **Painted Cave**.

The black tar (asphaltum) you may find on your feet after a trip to the beach seeped through the sand when Chumash lived along the shores. They used a less sticky tar found in beach and inland deposits to seal their inventive plank canoes (tomol). Constructed of driftwood planks hewn with shell and rock tools and strapped together with red milkweed, the canoes were so well designed that the only internal framing required was a single crossbar. A replica of the plank canoe, considered the greatest technical achievement of Pacific Coast Indians in North America, may be seen in the halls of the **County Courthouse**.

* Jimson Weed, also called "loco weed," is an indigenous plant to beware of: a doseage sufficient to cause hallucination borders on causing blindness and death.

Chumash Indian shaman.

THE SPANISH

A flurry of excitement spread through Chumash villages as the huge, billowing sails of two Spanish ships were spied across Channel waters in 1542. Indians paddled their tomol canoes out to greet the "mysterious winged" caravels of the Juan Rodriguez Cabrillo expedition. Cabrillo's landing is elaborately depicted in the lovely **Mural Room** of the **County Courthouse**, though his party did not come ashore in Santa Barbara at all. From his ship, the Portuguese navigator claimed the land for Spain and continued up the coast in search of a fabled passage to the Atlantic.

Though explorers passed through the area after Cabrillo (and perhaps before: Chumash legend suggests that a Chinese junk may have preceded them), the first permanent Spanish settlers did not arrive for over 200 years. A platoon of Spanish soldiers, accompanied by the founder of California's mission system, Padre Junipero Serra, was sent to establish a **Royal Presidio** as a Spanish military stronghold. This handful of *soldados de cuero* ("leather-jacketed soldiers," so-called for their heavy protective waistcoast of layered hide) was to protect Spanish interests in California from Los Angeles all the way to San Luis Obispo.

The Chumash helped the soldiers and their families to survive the early times before crops could be sown and harvested. The ingenuous Indian people were unaware that their culture would diminish to virtual extinction with the advent of white settlers and missionaries.

On an April morning in 1782, soldiers and Indians gathered with the grey-robed Padre Serra as a crude wooden cross was erected and blessed on the dusty flats near the site of the present main Post Office. As the United States was emerging a new nation from the Revolutionary War, the pueblo of Santa Barbara was officially founded.

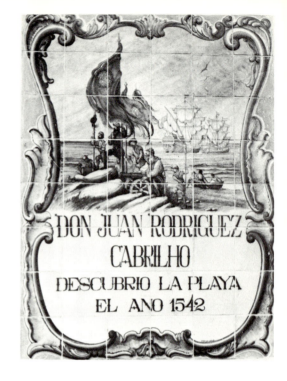

Cabrillo's landing depicted in tile at the Espana Restaurant. The explorer actually landed farther south in a smaller vessel than shown. Cabrillo may have ended his journey on nearby San Miguel Island where many believe he is buried.

Royal Spanish Presidio site shown in relation to modern streets of Santa Barbara.

Adobe homes of sun-dried earth and straw surrounded the Presidio.

ADOBE HOUSE

THE PRESIDIO

The fourth and final Royal Spanish Presidio in California (Spain's last military outpost to be built in the New World) began as a crude quadrangle of brush huts. Soldiers and Indians built barracks, officers' quarters and storehouses around a military parade ground. Quarters for the padres were built beside Santa Barbara's first church, the Presidio Chapel, which became the center of life in the young community. The temporary brush buildings were replaced by mud brick adobes with fieldstone foundations and roofs of fired clay tile.

Archaeological digs have uncovered the foundations of the Chapel and other early Presidio buildings. Santa Barbarans hope eventually to reconstruct the entire Presidio. You may wander through the excavations at 133 E. Canon Perdido St., where reconstruction of the Padres' Quarters has already begun.

Across the street at 122 E. Canon Perdido is **El Cuartel**, which means "The Guard's House." Constructed as part of the Presidio quadrangle in the 1780's, the restored El Cuartel is Santa Barbara's oldest surviving adobe.

OLD SPANISH DAYS

A pueblo of adobes sprouted around the Presidio as soldiers were joined by their families. Darkened by rawhide stretched over windows in lieu of glass, adobes had earthen floors with steers' blood added to make them harder. Beds were simply rawhide stretched over four poles, and they were among few other furnishings. With little for comfort indoors, many activities took place outside in the fresh air and sunshine.

Soldiers were poorly paid, fed and clothed. A Spanish supply ship came through the area only once a year and purchases from foreign vessels were forbidden. Under cover of darkness, American and other foreign vessels would anchor in nearby Refugio cove, often signalled from shore by lantern light. Trading went on through the night and the ships would leave before daybreak. Smuggling provided many of the basics and luxuries — from shoes and furnishings to fine Chinese silks — otherwise scarce or unavailable. The Presidio turned its eyes from the influx of much-needed contraband goods. As townspeople had little currency, they bartered with piles of stiff rawhide skins, known to many traders as "California currency."

Chumash woodcutter
and his wife, probably
the last Indian residents
of the Mission.
(Circa 1882)

"QUEEN OF THE MISSIONS"

Overlooking a maze of pueblo adobes, the Presidio, and the sea, the site for the new Mission was blessed on the Feast of St. Barbara, Dec. 4, 1786. Original thatch structures were replaced by adobes with huge pine log supports. As good wood was scarce, the heavy logs were carried by Mission Indians from as far away as 20 miles. It has been said that after blessing the logs, padres told Indians that the sacred logs must not touch the ground before reaching the Mission.

Fireworks lighted the evening skies over the newly completed Mission in 1833. Replacing earlier structures leveled by a devastating earthquake in 1812, the famed "Queen of the Missions" is crowned by the twin towers of a classic Roman chapel. Its design was inspired by a Mission-owned book of ancient Roman architecture, Vitruvius' *Six Books of Architecture*, written in 27 B.C. The classic chapel facade contrasts with low-slung tile-roofed extensions which surround lovely gardens.

Illustration by Western artist Alexander Harmer shows townsfolk returning from services at the newly completed Mission.

The Moorish fountain on the Mission piazza was originally fed by waters carried through stone aqueducts from an eleborate water system built by Mission Indians under the padres' guidance. (Remains of the stone aqueducts are still visible in the field across from the Mission.) Overflow from the fountain poured into the long stone *lavanderia*, or washing trough, where Indian women paddled their clothes against its rolled stone lip and rinsed them in the cool waters from above.

For a Chumash Indian, conversion by the missionaries meant abandoning a lifestyle and traditions of centuries to adopt the vastly different ways of Mission life. The introduction of Spanish culture affected the Chumash perception of the world and many Indians felt they would increase their spiritual powers through worship of the Spanish deity. Donning scant though unaccustomed clothing, they moved from their tule grass huts in Chumash villages to one room adobes beside the Mission. Indians who chose to enter Mission life lived and worked under the strict control of the padres. They were much better-treated by the missionaries than their unconverted peers were by the soldiers outside the Mission; however, Mission Indians relinquished their freedom along with their customs, and were no longer able to come and go as they pleased. Young girls were locked in a dormitory each night to ensure their virtue and families were allowed only occasional visits to their villages to see relatives and friends.

All Indian Mission band.

Over 4000 Indians, though less than half of the local Chumash population, were baptized by the missionaries. Indian neophytes farmed in Mission orchards and gardens, fashioned clay pots and utensils, ground grain in the Mission gristmill, tanned and crafted leather, learned carpentry and Spanish building methods, and women wove fabrics with handspun fibers. A few were even taught to play musical instruments for a curious-looking all Indian Mission band.

Abrupt changes in lifestyle, ill-treatment by the Spaniards and the arrival of European diseases, eventually broke the spirit and health of the Chumash people, both in and outside of the Mission. In the small Mission cemetery beside the chapel, 4000 Indians are buried. The Mission system flourished during the Spanish period, weathered cutbacks in wealth and power under the Mexicans and ended with secularization in 1833. By then, there were few of the original Chumash thousands, the most culturally advanced Indians of the California coast, who had survived the arrival of white settlers.

BUCCANEERS!

Revolt against Spain was spreading through her colonies in South and Central America when word reached Santa Barbara that Argentina had hired French buccaneer Hippolyte Bouchard and his 300 men to destroy Spanish ports all along the coast. The alarming news electrified the town: women and children were evacuated with valuables over San Marcos Pass, and *Comandante* Jose de la Guerra prepared with his men for the attack.

Bouchard's two black frigates dropped anchor in Refugio Bay while a band of soldiers and Mission Indians lay concealed on the shores nearby. The small band of men would have been little opposition to Bouchard's scores of buccaneers but, from their cover, they managed to lasso three of Bouchard's men who came ashore on a raid. The prisoners were marched to Santa Barbara in chains.

Days later, Bouchard set his spyglass on Santa Barbara and discovered a huge force of cavalry ready to defend the town. What he *actually* saw, was a handful of men riding around a thicket near the beach who changed clothes and horses when they were out of sight! Bouchard weighed the losses his own men might take against this ample force, and sent an ultimatum ashore: release his three men and he would set sail for other ports; otherwise, his heavy canons would bombard the pueblo to dust. The wise De la Guerra released the prisoners, and Bouchard sailed South, devastating San Juan Capistrano only days later.

THE MEXICANS

When the Mexican people successfully revolted against Spain, they took California along with them. The Spanish flag that had flown for forty years over Santa Barbara (1782-1822) was replaced by the Mexican eagle. Santa Barbara celebrated the *end* of old Spanish days with a huge town-wide fiesta. Dancing, feasting, horse racing, bear-and-bull fights, music, games and fireworks went on into the night.

José de la Guerra, the Spanish-born aristocrat who had been *Comandante* of the Spanish Presidio, pledged allegiance with other townspeople to the new Mexican government. The De la Guerras were the "first family" of Santa Barbara through Spanish and Mexican periods, and were still influential into the American era.

Casa de la Guerra, now part of the picturesque maze of shops and cafes of **El Paseo**, was the grandest house in town and the center of its social life. Lavish marriage celebrations for De la Guerra daughters were joined by the entire town. Houseguest Richard Henry Dana described the spirited life of Casa de la Guerra in his well-known book of travel, *Two Years Before the Mast*.

The 24 years of Mexican rule (1822-1846) eased the town from a Spanish military fortress into a domestic pueblo. Mission wealth & influence was reduced; trade restrictions with foreign vessels were relaxed; smuggling slackened; and a municipal government formed that served the town until the arrival of the Americans.

"LOST WOMAN OF SAN NICOLAS ISLAND"

In 1836 it was decided that Channel Island Chumash Indians, whose forefathers had lived on the isles for centuries, should be brought to the mainland. A ship was dispatched for that purpose and the entire tiny population of San Nicolas boarded to leave the island. As the ship set sail in a brewing storm, a young child was suddenly discovered missing and his mother leaped ashore to search for him. The storm swelled and the ship's captain decided not to risk staying to rescue them. A later vessel sent to recover the woman and child searched unsuccessfully.

It was 17 years later that Captain George Nidever and his men combed the island after finding indications of human habitation. After nearly two decades of a Robinson Crusoe existence, the woman (her child's fate is unknown) was discovered living in a cave, bedecked with bird feathers and existing primarily on fish, nuts and other gathered edibles. The woman readily accompanied the Captain back to the mainland where she was royally received. Speaking a language unfamiliar to other Chumash, the woman communicated with gestures. Despite her pleasure at being reunited with others, the homecoming did not benefit her health. The rich foods served in honor of her return upset her spartanly-accustomed system, and the woman of San Nicolas Island died weeks later.

THE AMERICANS

A popular image of Johnston McCulley's dashing fictional character, Zorro. McCulley's tales were based on local folk hero and bandit, Salomon Pico.

As the young, ambitious Americans stretched their ideal of "manifest destiny" to the west, they eventually reached the California coast. Unlike the Mexican takeover, American rule was not celebrated.

Expecting to ceremoniously lower the Mexican flag and raise the stars and stripes on his arrival in 1846, American Commodore Robert Stockton found that the Mexican flag had disappeared. A search of the town did not turn up the banner, which had been taken by the patriotic young wife of the Presidio commander. Hiding it in a trunk in her room, the young woman concealed it from the American soldiers who came to search by sitting on the trunk and spreading her skirts across it. Years later, however, she gave the historic banner away to be made into a peasant skirt.

As soon as American troops left behind to establish martial law were removed from the "sleepy" town, Mexican patriots burned the American flag and threatened the lives of American townspeople. Over 400 troops, led by Lt. Col. John Fremont, marched across San Marcos Pass in a torrential downpour to recapture Santa Barbara. Since many of the town's men were off fighting in the South, Fremont's more-than-ample force took the town without firing a shot.

CANON PERDIDO (The Lost Cannon)

Canon Perdido Street takes its name from a curious incident that needled the Americans. Among the salvage on West Beach from a shipwreck years earlier was an inoperative brass cannon. A few young Santa Barbarans borrowed an oxcart one night to drag the cannon to a hiding place near the Salt Pond (now the Bird Refuge). Along the way, the cannon sank in a bog of quicksand on East Beach.

News of its disappearance alarmed the local American commander, who frantically petitioned the governor for military support to quell an imagined uprising. Rather than sending troops, the governor levied a $500 fine on the people of Santa Barbara, to be collected unless the cannon was returned.

Worried that this would rock the already shaky peace with Santa Barbarans, the Captain threw a July 4th celebration for the townspeople. After apologetically explaining his dilemma to the festive gathering of Santa Barbarans, the American leader passed a hat which was quickly filled to pay the fine.

A storm ten years later uncovered the missing cannon, but the young conspirators were much older before any revealed their late night escapade.

ZORRO

The bandit and folk hero whose legend was romantically fictionalized in the dashing, black-caped figure of "Zorro" (the Fox) was a handsome local aristocrat whose rancho was in the nearby Santa Ynez Valley.

Salomon Pico, a cousin of Governor Pio Pico and member of California's richest and most powerful family, was robbed and beaten by a gang of Americans. The vendetta that he carried embodied the resentments of many Spanish-speaking Californians toward the overtaking *Yanquis*. Salomon Pico led his band of followers in roadside ambushes of "gringos" traveling along the King's Highway (El Camino Real, which follows much the same route as Hwy. 101). He relieved them of purses which often jangled heavily from cattle trading with rich gold rush towns to the North. (Gold miners readily paid as much as an ounce of gold — $19 — for a 10 oz. steak!) Rather than leaving the slashing mark of Zorro with the zip! zip! zip! of his sword, Pico's more gruesome trademark was to remove his victims' ears and string them on a leather thong. It is said that the grim collection was intended as a gift for a ladyfriend.

Johnston McCulley, who began the popular series of novels about "Zorro" in 1919, realized that his American readers would have little sympathy with a hero who robbed and murdered Americans. He wisely set back the clock and changed the setting to a Mexican town where the villains were Spanish aristocrats and soldiers.

The folk hero, who seemed to many a common bandit, was protected from capture and prosecution by powerful supporters until at last he fled to Mexico. Salomon Pico's saddle is in the Santa Barbara Historical Museum.

STREETS

Well-worn pathways that meandered through adobes surrounding the Presidio became the first of Santa Barbara's streets.

In 1851 a surveyor was sought to create order in the town's layout. A steamboat skipper named Salisbury Haley won the honors, but his methods in carrying out the survey proved questionable. For reasons unknown, Haley alligned the streets at a diagonal to both the coast and the four points of the compass. Also his measurements were found to be inaccurate: in places the streets were as much as 45 feet out of allignment. Many believe that Haley used leather straps to mend breaks in his measuring chain. Since leather expands on foggy days and contracts when it is dry and hot, hide is not the most reliable choice for such patchwork. When the Haley Survey was completed, several of the town's adobes were in the middle of the new streets. In an attempt to untangle the confusion created by the Haley Survey, a later survey was undertaken. Much of Santa Barbara's layout, however, still reflects the surveying skill of Salisbury Haley.

Christened with a colorful array of Spanish and Indian names from the town's romantic past, the streets, shown in this 1888 lithograph, reflect a character and history unique to Santa Barbara.

STAGECOACHES

The whole town of twelve hundred came out to greet the first stagecoach to come over San Marcos Pass in 1861. The Pass was so steep in places that horizonal ruts had to be carved in the rock, washboard style, to keep the coaches from rolling back down. Passengers often had to tote their baggage up that leg of the journey. Mail was soon delivered by stagecoach, but the trained horses were not stopped between destinations. Drivers would toss a packet of mail to the local postal official while galloping past. As the horses ran in a full circle, the clerk quickly sorted the mail to toss back outgoing mail when the stagecoach passed by again.

Mattei's Tavern in Los Olivos is a former stagecoach stop where travellers may still relax for an evening meal. **Cold Springs Tavern**, a rustic pub and restaurant on Stagecoach Rd. off San Marcos Pass (154), is another vintage establishment which is widely thought to have served as a resting place along the stagecoach trail.

TIPS FOR STAGECOACH TRAVELLERS

As many as 18 people packed into the small wooden coaches that climbed San Marcos Pass to and from Santa Barbara. Nine could ride inside while the other nine were clinging on top. Bumps and bounces were lessened only by layered strips of leather that acted as springs. The following suggestions to stagecoach travellers were included in an article published in the Omaha Herald, Oct. 3, 1871:

The best seat inside a stage is the one next to the driver. Even if you have a tendency to seasickness when riding backwards, you will get less jolts and jostling.

When the driver asks you to get off and walk, do so without grumbling. If the team runs away, sit still and take your chances. If you jump, nine out of ten times you will get hurt.

In cold weather don't ride with tight-fitting boots, shoes or gloves. In very cold weather abstain entirely from liquor when on the road, because you freeze twice as quickly when under the influence.

Don't smoke a strong pipe inside the coach; spit on the leeward side. If you have anything to drink in a bottle, pass it around. Procure your stimulants before starting, as "ranch" (Stage Depot) whiskey is not "nectar".

Don't swear or lop over neighbors when sleeping. Take small change to pay expenses. Never shoot on the road as the noise might frighten horses. Don't discuss politics or religion. Don't point out where murders have been committed, especially if there are women passengers.

Don't lag at the wash basin. Don't grease your hair, because travel is dusty.

Don't imagine for a moment that you are going on a picnic. Expect annoyances, discomfort, and some hardship.

THE BLOOM OF THE 1870's

Santa Barbara blossomed in the 1870's. Its fame as a health resort spread through the world, greatly heralded for the healing properties of Montecito's Hot Springs (now part of the village's water system).

John Stearns built a 1500-foot wharf that stretched out to meet ocean-going vessels, opening Santa Barbara as a seaport. (Before that time, passengers were often carried ashore on the shoulders of brawny sailors. If they did not provide a suitable tip, however, they were likely to be dunked!)

A gifted Italian musician named Jose Lobero, a newcomer with an intriguingly mysterious past, opened Southern California's first opera house in the heart of Santa Barbara's Chinatown. The largest adobe structure in California, the Lobero Opera Theater had a balcony ingeniously suspended from the ceiling so columns would not obstruct the view of patrons.

A wealthy sheep baron named Colonel W. W. Hollister saw the influx of health-seekers as an opportunity to profit in the hotel business. The fabulous Arlington Hotel was built on the site of the present **Arlington Center for the Performing Arts**. With five acres of surrounding deer and rose gardens, panoramic ocean views from grand piazzas, and fireplaces in each of its 90 luxuriously furnished rooms, the Arlington amply catered to its wealthy clientele. Horse-drawn streetcars carried guests arriving at Stearns Wharf up State Street to the Arlington, or to another, more modest, Hollister-owned hotel. Residents frequently saw Colonel Hollister on Stearns Wharf, greeting visitors as ships came to port. It is said that he noted their visible means, and directed them accordingly to one of his two hotels.

An unheralded event of the 1870's led to the most amazing growth in Santa Barbara's history. A young girl planted a seedling, given to her by a sailor just back from Australia, and it grew into the enormous twisting limbs and huge leafy canopy of the **Moreton Bay Fig Tree**. Believed to be the largest of its species in the world, its roots stretch over an entire acre. Though its branches are kept pruned to 160 ft., it is estimated that 10,000 people could stand in its shade at noon. The 100 year old fig tree, saved from the woodcutter's ax by town outcry (it was to be chopped down in the 30's to make way for a gas station), has never grown a fig. Merely a relative of fig-bearing trees, it is also a relative of the popular household rubber plant.

STREETCARS

Horse-drawn cars, that had carried passengers up State St. since 1876, were replaced with electric streetcars near the turn of the century. The route that they travelled, from Stearns Wharf to the Arlington Hotel, was lengthened to reach the Mission. It continued from there up the gently graded curves of Alameda Padre Serra, designed especially to be negotiated by the streetcars.

Competition from the automobile ended the era of the streetcar in 1929.

FILMING THE STARS

In the early days of filmmaking, Santa Barbara bustled with actors, cameramen and directors, filming thousands of scenes that flickered across the young silver screen. Model T's, with cameramen cranking their early cameras, followed the action as actors played out scenes on Santa Barbara's streets. The hills and chapparal around San Marcos Pass stirred with gunfights and Indian raids. Montecito's luxurious homes became Spanish haciendas, French chateaux, castles and villas, with dramas unfolding at their doorsteps.

Over a dozen studios sprang up, one of which, built in 1913, led the field briefly as the largest movie studio in the world. For that short time, Santa Barbara reigned as the capital of the film industry.

Big city settings drew early filmmakers to young Hollywood, a better-known movie capital, but Santa Barbara's sun-swept coast, tile-roofed white buildings, and lovely homes are still backdrops of occasional television and film productions. A film haven in another sense, Santa Barbara and its environs have become the home of several famous entertainers, directors and producers, as well as artists, writers and musicians.

CHINATOWN

Canon Perdido Street, near the present Post Office, was the heart of a bustling Chinatown for over fifty years. Fan-tan parlors, oriental markets, shops and laundries lined the streets where secret societies called "Tongs" ruled the gambling dens, opium trade and "protection" interests.

The clashing of two powerful Tongs over the control of a shared gambling house erupted in a Tong war in the mid-20's. A young attorney was retained and briefed on behalf of his murder clients *before* a murder had actually taken place. As a score of evening theater-goers filed from a nearby performance, two Chinese hitmen gunned down the Tong leader as he exited the gambling house.

The two gunmen were tracked to a barn on the outskirts of town and arrested. In spite of the massive evidence and dozens of witnesses, the attorney managed to get his clients off. He demanded that his clients be positively identified in a lineup. After studying the row of Chinese faces, witnesses were unable to pick out the gunmen, and the men were released.

This last eruption marked the close of an era, and Chinatown has since disappeared. An elaborate hand-carved Chinese shrine in the **Santa Barbara Historical Museum** is one of the last indications of the community's flourish.

Hand-carved Chinese shrine in the Santa Barbara Historical Museum.

"OLD SPANISH DAYS" REVIVED

Interest in Santa Barbara's Spanish heritage was rekindled in the 1920's. **El Paseo**, a charming arcade of tile-roofed shops and cafes joined by flagstone walkways, was built adjacent to historic **Casa de la Guerra**, by a patron of Spanish redevelopment, Bernhard Hoffman. The grand reopening of the rebuilt **Lobero Theater** was celebrated with a week-long fiesta, beginning the popular annual fiesta tradition that honors Santa Barbara's "Old Spanish Days".

From the late 1800's, adobes were replaced by wooden clapboard Victoriana that characterized towns throughout the Old West. By the twentieth century, much of it was unattractive and in need of repair, but city planners felt they had years ahead of them before the old could be replaced by the new. An unexpected occurence changed that abruptly.

Scenes after the powerful quake of 1925. Above left, walls of the newly opened Hotel California peeled from their frame leaving a honeycomb of open guest rooms. Rubble spilled into State St. above and to the right is a view of the demolished San Marcos Building.

EARTHQUAKE!

At 6:42 on the morning of June 29, 1925, Santa Barbarans were jolted awake by the violent trembling of floors and walls, shattering glass and the rumbling growl of shifting earth. Earthquake tremors from shifts along the More Ranch and Mesa faults, reaching 6.3 on the Richter scale, began a permanent rearrangement of the face of Santa Barbara.

The Old Mission towers tumbled to the ground. Storefronts and hotel facades peeled from their frames, leaving startled hotel patrons staring from their beds to the street below. Rubble spilled into the streets. Thirteen people died. In just nineteen seconds, it was over, and Downtown Santa Barbara was virtually destroyed.

The powerful quake flattened a hodge-podge of flimsy structures, leaving the newer and sturdier buildings intact. The cleared slate was taken as an opportunity for a fresh start, and an Architectural Board of Review formed to guide Santa Barbara toward a unity of style based on her Spanish past. From the rubble of the quake, white stucco buildings sprouted throughout town with clay-tiled roofs, graceful archways and colorful inlaid tiles.

SANTA BARBARA COUNTY COURTHOUSE

The loveliest single result of the powerful earthquake was the new County Courthouse, built on the site of its razed predecessor. Lines of stone foundation from the earlier Courthouse still border the attractively landscaped Sunken Gardens. From Anacapa Street, the gardens are framed by Anacapa Arch, hand-fashioned of Refugio sandstone and chiseled in Spanish with the motto: "God Gave Us the Country, the Skill of Man Hath Built the Town."

It was the skill of architect William Mooser, many fine craftsmen and Mooser's son, back from a 17-year stay in Spain, that created the palace-like Spanish-Moorish Courthouse. Completed in 1929 (just before the Stock Market crash) at a cost of $1,500,000, the Santa Barbara Courthouse was hailed an artistic triumph.

Imaginative groupings of individually-shaped windows, curving indoor/outdoor staircases, open-air balconies, romantic turrets and archways are brought together in a masterly blend of architectural sculpture. Mooser whimsically added a turret, facing Santa Barbara Street, that has no entrance or exit. Beneath the turret is carved the face of a laughing man.

The off-center placements of arch-within-arch, scattered window openings in unmatched shapes and sizes and only rare elements of classical symmetry, reflect the influence of the Moors, who felt that man's works should not mirror God-like perfection. Avoiding also the use of human and animal images, Moorish influence can be seen in the colorful, inlaid Tunisian tiles patterning hallways.

Each interior element has been carefully selected for its craftsmanship and design, from wrought iron hallway lanterns, said to be copied from lanterns of Spanish ships, to the detailed ceiling supports, many of which are quake-resistant, reinforced concrete, molded to look like wooden beams. Doors-within-doors, used in Spanish castles to accomodate both carriages and pedestrians, gate some entrances. Other carved doors appeared of too recent vintage to architect Mooser, and so he buried them in his mother's garden, watering them regulary, until they took on the aged appearance he desired.

Artist Dan Sayre Groesbeck, experienced in creating vast scenarios as backdrops for Hollywood's Cecil B. DeMille, has retold stories of Santa Barbara's past in the second floor Mural Room. The hand-screened ceiling design over the colorfully tiled nearby staircase is a replica of one gracing a synagog in Toledo, Spain.

From a perch in El Mirador clock tower 70 ft. up (reached by elevator), visitors are surrounded by ocean, mountains and terra cotta rooftops stretching to the sea. The directional diagram on the floor helps in getting bearings with Santa Barbara's confusing East-West coastline and diagonal city streets. On a clear day the Channel Islands rise above the horizon; when it is overcast, however, they often live up to the Indian name given to the most easterly isle, Anacapa, which implies that it vanishes like a mirage.

The observation deck
in the clock tower of the
Santa Barbara County
Courthouse offers rooftop
views (left) and a
panorama of the city.
Below is the Mural Room
with scenes of
Santa Barbara's past.

HIGHLIGHTS

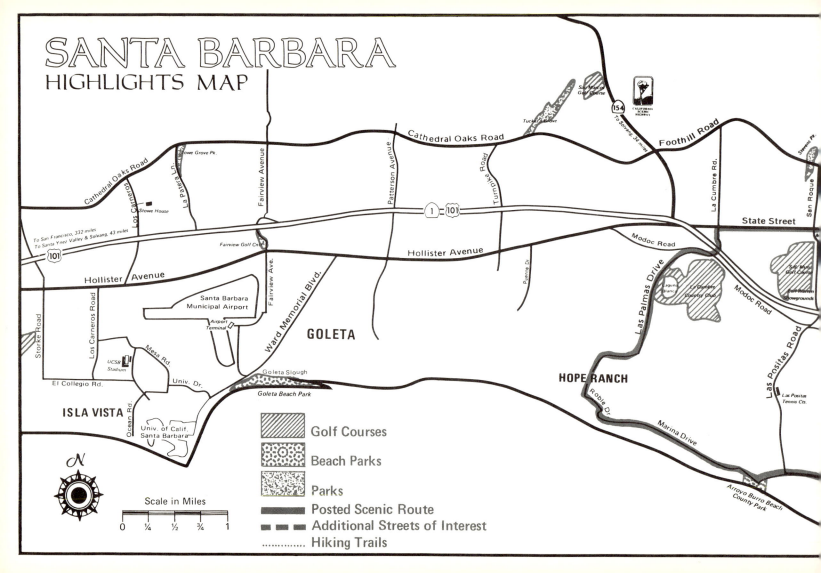

SANTA BARBARA
HIGHLIGHTS MAP

San Marcos Golf Course

Tucker's Grove

154
To Solvang, 34 miles

CALIFORNIA SCENIC HIGHWAY

Cathedral Oaks Road

Foothill Road

Stowe Grove Pk.

Cathedral Oaks Road

La Patera Ln.

Los Carneros

Stowe House

Fairview Avenue

Patterson Avenue

Turnpike Road

La Cumbre Rd.

Stewart Pk.

San Roque

1 101

State Street

To San Francisco, 332 miles
To Santa Ynez Valley & Solvang, 43 miles

101

Fairview Golf Cntr.

Hollister Avenue

Modoc Road

San Marcos Golf Course

Earl Warren Showgrounds

Hollister Avenue

Fairview Ave.

Ward Memorial Blvd.

Puente Dr.

Laguna Blanca

La Cumbre Country Club

Modoc Road

Las Palmas Drive

Santa Barbara
Municipal Airport

Airport
Terminal

GOLETA

Storke Road

Los Carneros Road

Mesa Rd.

UCSB
Stadium

Univ. Dr.

Goleta Slough

HOPE RANCH

Las Positas Road

Las Positas Tennis Cts.

El Collegio Rd.

Goleta Beach Park

Roble Dr.

Ocean Rd.

ISLA VISTA

Univ. of Calif.
Santa Barbara

Marina Drive

Arroyo Burro Beach
County Park

N

Scale in Miles
0   ¼   ½   ¾   1

	Legend
	Golf Courses
	Beach Parks
	Parks
	Posted Scenic Route
	Additional Streets of Interest
....	Hiking Trails

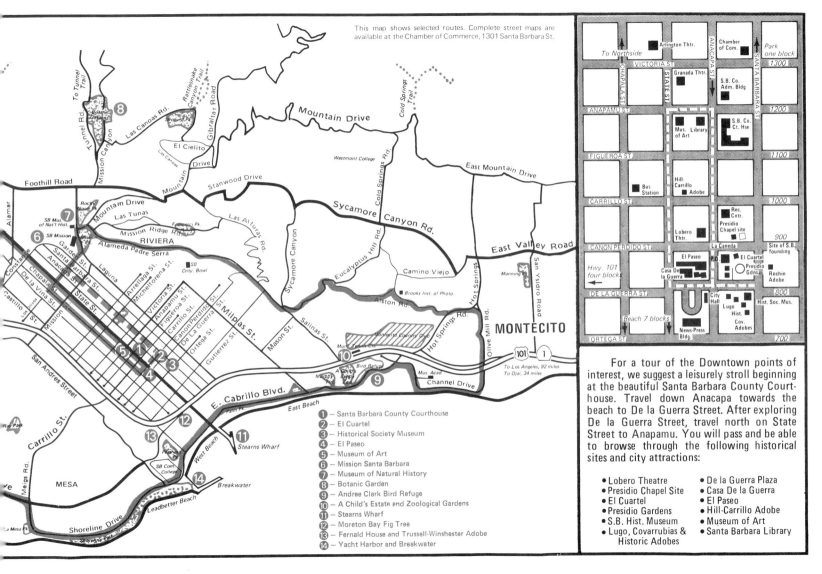

This map shows selected routes. Complete street maps are available at the Chamber of Commerce, 1301 Santa Barbara St.

MONTECITO

1 — Santa Barbara County Courthouse
2 — El Cuartel
3 — Historical Society Museum
4 — El Paseo
5 — Museum of Art
6 — Mission Santa Barbara
7 — Museum of Natural History
8 — Botanic Garden
9 — Andree Clark Bird Refuge
10 — A Child's Estate and Zoological Gardens
11 — Stearns Wharf
12 — Moreton Bay Fig Tree
13 — Fernald House and Trussell-Winshester Adobe
14 — Yacht Harbor and Breakwater

For a tour of the Downtown points of interest, we suggest a leisurely stroll beginning at the beautiful Santa Barbara County Courthouse. Travel down Anacapa towards the beach to De la Guerra Street. After exploring De la Guerra Street, travel north on State Street to Anapamu. You will pass and be able to browse through the following historical sites and city attractions:

- Lobero Theatre
- Presidio Chapel Site
- El Cuartel
- Presidio Gardens
- S.B. Hist. Museum
- Lugo, Covarrubias & Historic Adobes
- De la Guerra Plaza
- Casa De la Guerra
- El Paseo
- Hill-Carrillo Adobe
- Museum of Art
- Santa Barbara Library

The scene below right is an entry in the annual summer sandcastle contest held at East Beach. Other annual ocean happenings include Semina Nautica in July with a score of sailing and sporting events and the popular King's Harbor Race in August.

OCEAN

Miles of free public beaches stretch along the Santa Barbara shores. The sparkling blue waters are inviting to sailors, deep sea divers and fishermen, swimmers and sunbathers, surfers and all who enjoy the beauty and mystery of the ocean.

Sailing and Boating

Sailed by Spaniards, smugglers, pirates, Russian otter hunters, whalers and fishermen the waters of the Santa Barbara Channel have challenged many a hardy crew. Winds sweeping down the California coast whip around the land's bend at Point Conception, the tip of a 50-mile stretch of East-West coastline. Gusts often gather the force of gales as they race along the skirt of the four nearby Channel Islands — San Miguel, Santa Rosa, Santa Cruz and Anacapa — that rim the 25-mile Channel corridor.

Many who sail to the islands are caught in a blustery 6-mile strip just off the isles known

as "Windy Lane." It is recommended that those visiting the islands stay the night if waters are rough, since they will be doubly challenging out in "Windy Lane."

Calmer waters along the Santa Barbara shores are dotted with sails on sunny afternoons. Weather patterns change quickly as afternoon winds pick up from the morning calm. The sailing season for most is May through October, though sailors skilled in handling challenging winds enjoy sailing the Channel all year round.

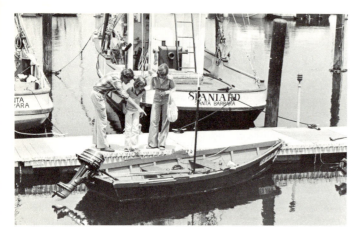

Boat Rentals

Santa Barbara Boat Rentals
Launch ramp at Breakwater, 962-2826
West Beach Marine Co.
Marina 2 at Breakwater, 963-5600
Sailing school, rentals, charters, sales.
Goleta Beach Sport Fishing
Goleta Beach Park, 967-2104
Pier and boating facilities. Bait & tackle.
Cachuma Lake Recreation Area
24 miles via Hwy 154, 1-688-4040
Rowboats & motorboats, fishing, camping hiking, picnics, 18-hole miniature golf course, swimming in pools, riding stables.
Pedal Power Boat Co.
West Beach across from Sambos. Daily summer pedal boat rentals for 1-2 persons. Discount tickets at motels.

Scuba Diving

Divers Den
22 Anacapa Street, 963-8917
Sales & rentals of wet suits, regulators, backpacks, weights, buoyancy compensators. Also offers a full program of diving lessons and activities including: scuba classes in their indoor training pool, underwater photography, excursions to the islands for shipwreck diving and night diving.

Fishing

Deep sea and surf fishing throughout the year. Pacific red snapper, rock cod, swordfish and halibut. Pier fishing at Goleta Pier. Bait & tackle available at the Breakwater and Goleta Pier. Fishing map for general areas of coastal, island and inland fishing spots available at Chamber of Commerce, 1301 Santa Barbara St.

Sea Landing
Pier at Cabrillo and Bath 963-3564
Year-round island & coastal fishing. Bait and tackle shop.
Goleta Beach Sport Fishing
5905 Sandspit Rd. at Goleta Beach, 967-2104; 967-5427
Outer island fishing year-round, live bait, boat charters, rentals, bait & tackle shop.
Cachuma Lake
See BOAT RENTALS. Bass fishing.

Surfing

Beaches in the Santa Barbara vicinity, like those throughout Southern California, draw flocks of enthusiastic surfers. Rincon Point, southeast of Carpinteria, is known throughout the state as an excellent surfing spot for those skilled in the sport. Other beaches attract surfers with varying skills, from beginners to dedicated veterans.

In wintertime surf is at its highest and beach floors tend to be rocky. Water temperatures average: 56°-57° Nov-March; 58°-60° April-May; 62°-65° June-Aug; and 59°-60° Sept-Oct.

Surfboards, in limited supply, may be rented at the following locations (call in advance):

Surf 'n Wear — 209 W. Carrillo, 963-3213
Channel Islands Surfboards — 16 Helena Ave., 966-7213

Surfing Beaches	Bottom (summer)	Average Wave Ht. (ft.) Summer	Winter	Max. Wave Ht.	Surfing Ability	Lifeguard (summer)
Rincon Point	rocky	1	3-4	8-10	A	No
Carpinteria	sandy	1-2	3	4-6	B-I	Yes
Summerland	sandy	1	1	3-6	B-I	Yes
Leadbetter Bch	sand & rock	1	1-3	4-6	B	No
Arroyo Burro	sand, some rock	1-3	2-4	4-6	B-A	Yes
UCSB	sand, some rock	1-3	3-4	6-8	B-A	No
El Capitan Bch	sandy	1-3	2-4	6-7	B-A	Yes
El Capitan Point	rocky	1-3	2-4	6-7	A	No
Refugio	rocky	1-2	2-4	4-6	B-A	Yes

B-Beginner I-Intermediate A-Advanced

INLAND

Bicycling

Open Air Bicycles
8 W. Cabrillo Blvd., 963-2524
Bicycle rentals, motorized bicycles,
rollerskates.

Bowling

San Marcos Lanes
4050 Calle Real, 967-5631
32 lanes, cocktail lounge, billiards.
Orchid Bowl
5925 Calle Real, 967-0128
24 lanes, lounge, billiards, coffee shop.
Open 24 hours.

Lawn Bowling:

MacKenzie Park
State & De la Vina, 687-9069
Mon/Wed/Fri/Sat, 12:30-4:30 pm.
Spencer Adams Park
Anapamu & De la Vina, 965-9448
Tues/Thurs/Sat/Sun, 12:30-4:30 pm.

Fishing

See OCEAN (inland fishing included).

Folkdancing

Everyone welcome to join free
folkdancing Weds. 8-10pm at Oak Park
or Sundays 3-5pm at Palm Park.

Golf

Santa Barbara Community Course
Las Positas & McCaw Ave., 687-7087
18-holes, club & electric cart rentals,
putting green, driving range. Open
daily 6am to dark.
San Marcos Pass Course
1187 Via Chaparral, 967-3901
9-holes, clubs & electric cart rentals,
putting green. Daily 8am-7pm.
Fairview Community Golf Center
6034 Hollister Ave., Goleta, 964-1414
9-holes, par 3. Club rentals, driving
range, night lights, putting green. Daily
8am-10pm.
University Village Golf Center
Storke Rd., S. of 101, Goleta, 968-6814
9-holes, club rentals, driving range,
elec. carts, putting green. Weekdays
8am-dark; weekends 6:30am-dark.
Sandpiper Golf Course
7925 Hollister, Goleta, 968-1541
18-holes, regulation course, club &
cart rentals, putting green, driving
range. Weekdays 7:30am-dark;
weekends 6:30am-dark.

Miniature Golf:

Golf & Fun
401 Hitchcock Way (La Cumbre exit
off Hwy..101), 687-8485
Attractive miniature course, game
arcade, snack bar, skateboard park.

Hang Gliding

Channel Islands Hang Glider Emporium
613 N. Milpas, 965-3733
Instruction available (18 & over),
equipment provided.

Horses

Cachuma Trail Riding Stables
1 mi. w. of entrance to Cachuma Lake
Recreation area, 1-688-3018
Call for times and reservations.
Gene O'Hagen Stables
20 miles north of Santa Barbara along
Hwy. 101, Refugio State Beach exit, 3½
miles inland. 968-5929
Two hour scenic rides to waterfalls.
Parties of 4 or more may arrange early
evening rides. Reservations.
Rancho Oso Stables
12 miles from S.B. on Hwy. 154,
5 miles right on Paradise Rd. 967-4155
Escorted mountain trailrides. Weekend
breakfast rides. Reservations.
San Ysidro Ranch Stables
900 San Ysidro Lane, 969-5046
Scenic mountain trailrides from historic
guest ranch. Instruction available.

Picnics

See PARKS.

Polo

Pologrounds
Hwy. 101 near Carpinteria, 684-5819
Trophy matches can be seen on Sundays,
practice matches on Saturdays.

Sailing & Boating

See OCEAN.

Scuba Diving

See OCEAN.

Skating

The Ice Patch
1933 Cliff Drive, 963-0833
Indoor ice rink for day and evening
public skating. Call for information on
special programs, lessons & hours.
Entrance fee and skate rentals.
Open Air Bicycles
8 W. Cabrillo, 963-2524
Soft-wheeled outdoor roller skates
available for cruising around the beach.
Day and evening rentals.
High Rollers
322 W. Cabrillo Blvd., 965-5985
Soft-wheeled outdoor roller skates.
Group rates.
Santa Barbara Rollercade
25 W. Gutierrez St., 962-6613
Indoor roller rink. Music and snack bar.
Entrance fees include skates.
Goleta Rollercade
6466 Hollister Ave., 968-4392
Indoor rink. Pro shop, snack bar,
instruction available.

Skateboard Parks

Golf & Fun
401 Hitchcock Way, 687-0735
Sparks Goleta Skateboard
360 Storke Rd., Goleta, 968-4257

Swimming

Free public beaches stretching along the
coast.
Municipal Outdoor Pools: (small fee)
—W. Cabrillo Blvd. & Castillo St.,
June-Sept 1-5pm daily.
—Ortega Park, 600 E. Ortega,
June-Sept, Tues-Thurs 3-5pm,
Sat & Sun 12-5.

Tennis

Call 963-0461 to inquire about permits
for city courts.
Pershing Park (8 courts)
W. Cabrillo & Castillo St.
Municipal Courts (12 courts)
1414 Park Pl. (Old Coast Hwy. near 101
and Salinas) 966-5255
Las Positas Municipal Courts (6 courts)
1002 Las Positas Rd. 687-2560
Night lights.

Volleyball

See PARKS.

Wagon Tours

Sunburst Organic Farms offers free
horsedrawn wagon tours of Tajiguas
Ranch. Call well in advance for
reservations. 968-6413

Wine Tasting & Winery Tours

Santa Barbara Winery
202 Anacapa, 963-8924
Firestone Vineyard
Zaca Station Road (near Foxen
Canyon Rd), Los Olivos, 688-3940

ANNUAL EVENTS

Old Spanish Days Fiesta

Santa Barbara's annual summer fiesta commemorating its Spanish heritage draws hundreds of thousands of visitors each year. First celebrated in 1924 with the opening of the new Lobero Theater, the Old Spanish Days Fiesta has been interrupted only by the earthquake of 1925 and the war years of World War II.

Fiesta commences on a Wednesday in August and continues through the following Sunday. Parades, carnivals, rodeos, dancing in the streets and on the waterfront, a Spanish marketplace in De la Guerra Plaza (El Mercado), arts and crafts shows on the beach and evening entertainment in the Courthouse sunken gardens are fiesta traditions. El Desfile Historico, the Old Spanish Days Parade, takes place on Thursday afternoon beginning on the beach at the foot of State St. and travelling up Castillo to Haley, east to State St. and up State to Sola. The Saturday morning El Desfile de Los Ninos, the Children's Parade, has become a Fiesta favorite. For a complete schedule of events, visit the Chamber of Commerce, 1301 Santa Barbara St. at Victoria.

Month	Event	Location
January	Antique Show & Sale	EWS
March or April	Santa Barbara Easter Relays	
	Arabian Horse Show	EWS
	Cymbidium Orchid Show	EWS
	Channel City Horse Show	EWS
	Mineral & Gem Show	EWS
May	Arabian Horse Show	EWS
	La Purisma Mission Fiesta	Lompoc
June	Elks' Rodeo & Parade	Santa Maria
	Jaycee's Community Fair	EWS
	Royal Lipizzan Stallion Show	EWS
	Lompoc Flower Festival	Lompoc
	S.B. Summer Sports Festival	
July	S.B. Nat'l Horse & Flower Show	EWS
	Summer Music Festival Series	
	Coin Show	EWS
	S.B. County Fair	Santa Maria
July & August	Solvang Theaterfest	Solvang
August	FIESTA "Old Spanish Days"	
	King Harbor Race	
	Morgan Horse Show	EWS
September	Danish Days	Solvang
	Arabian Horse Show	EWS
	Antique Show & Sale	EWS
November	BSA Fun Fair	EWS
	S.B Nat'l Amateur Horse Show	EWS

EWS — Earl Warren Showgrounds, Las Positas exit of Hwy. 101

Fiesta dancer.

GARDENS & PARKS

Botanic Gardens   Adm. Free
1212 Mission Canyon Rd. (1.5 miles N. of Old Mission)
Daily 8am-sunset; Guided tours Thurs. 10:30am
Seventy-five acres of native California plantlife with five miles of pleasant hiking trails. California golden poppy, redwoods, wild flowers and cactus gardens. Brilliant with color in spring. Historic dam built by Mission Indians in 1806, part of an elaborate Mission water system constructed under the direction of the padres.

A Child's Estate and Zoological Gardens
1300 E. Cabrillo Blvd. (East of Milpas St.)
Tues-Sun 10am-5pm
Adm: Adults $1.25; Juniors (13-18) 75¢; Children (2-12) 50¢
Enchanting small zoo in a garden setting. Farm animals, exotic birds, elephants, lions, monkeys and seals are among its many residents. Brightly painted miniature train tours grounds that were once part of a fabulous estate. Views of the ocean, bird refuge and gibbon island. Pirate ship and Wild West play areas. Picnic spots and snack bar.

Andree Clark Bird Refuge   Adm. Free
1400 E. Cabrillo Blvd. (Parking along Los Patos Way, N. of lagoon)
Beautiful lagoon and gardens on reclaimed salt marshland. For years the pond was overlooked by a 'hobo jungle', its residents guests of the late Mrs. John Child of the neighboring estate (now the zoo). Now the pond is a haven for many varieties of visiting and resident wildfowl. Bike and footpaths circle the pond.

City Parks

	Softball	Baseball	Soccer	Botanical Collect.	Bowling Greens	Camping	Child's Play Equip.	Hiking	Horseshoes	Nightlights	Neighborhood Park	Picnic Tables	BBQ's or Fire Pits	Swimming Pools	Wading Pools	Putting Greens	Scenic	Shuffleboard	Tennis	Volleyball	Waterways	
Alameda Park				•						•	•						•					Gazebo, specimen trees & shrubs
Andree Clark Bird Refuge																	•				L O	Scenic, bikepaths
Cabrillo Ball Park	•							•														
De La Guerra Plaza																•						Friday 12:15 lunchtime mini-concerts
Dwight Murphy Field	•	•					•				•	•				•				•		Clubhouse, locker rooms, snack bar
East & West Beaches							•							•	•	•				•	O	Snack bar
Francesci Park			•				•				•	•				•						Scenic views
Hilda Ray Park							•			•	•	•				•						Scenic views
Las Positas Tennis Courts								•											•			Tennis permit policy
Leadbetter Beach										•	•	•				•				•	O	Snack bar
MacKenzie Park	•				•		•				•	•							•			
Mission Park				•												•						Rose gardens, historic Mission ruins
Municipal Tennis Courts																		•				Tennis permit policy
Oak Park							•		•	•	•	•	•		•		•	•			C	Weekly folk dancing on dance platform
Ortega Park	•								•	•	•	•		P	•			•				Dance pavillion
Palm Park		•									•		O		•						O	Sunday Arts & Crafts Show, folk dancing
Pershing Park		•								•	•	•						•	•			
Plaza del Mar											•	•									O	Concert bandshell
Rattlesnake Canyon								•														Ruggedly beautiful hiking
Shoreline Park						•					•	•				•					O	Panoramic views, kite flying
Skofield Park						•	•				•	•				•					C	Only city camping area (tent)
Spencer Adams Park					•						•				•	•						
Stevens Park							•	•			•					•				•	C	

County Parks

P - Pool   C - Creek
O - Ocean   L - Lagoon

	Softball	Baseball	Soccer	Botanical Collect.	Bowling Greens	Camping	Child's Play Equip.	Hiking	Horseshoes	Nightlights	Neighborhood Park	Picnic Tables	BBQ's or Fire Pits	Swimming Pools	Wading Pools	Putting Greens	Scenic	Shuffleboard	Tennis	Volleyball	Waterways	
Arroyo Burro Beach											•		O							•	O	Snack bar, surfing, surf fishing, tidepools
Goleta Beach Park							•				•	•	O							•	O	Boat rentals, bait & tackle shop, snack bar Pier fishing, group picnic areas
Manning Park	•						•		•							•		•	•			Gardens, group picnic sites
Rocky Nook Park							•				•	•									C	
Stowe Grove Park	•						•				•	•							•			S. California's only redwood grove, group picnic sites
Tucker's Grove							•	•			•	•								•	•	Group picnic facilities, equestrian & hiking trails

MUSEUMS

Santa Barbara Museum of Art   **Admission Free**
1130 State St. (at Anapamu); 963-4364
Tues-Sat 11am-5pm; Sun noon-5pm; Closed Mondays
Attractive, growing Museum with a fine permanent collection, including: Pre-Columbian sculpture, Oriental art and musical instruments, African sculpture, a doll collection and American and European paintings. New and changing visiting exhibits. Free guided tours, Tues-Fri at 12:30 and 2:00. Classic and children's films scheduled.

Museum of Natural History   **Admission Free**
2559 Puesta del Sol Rd. (Follow signs along Mission Canyon Rd., 2 blks. N. of Santa Barbara Mission) 682-4711
Mon-Sat 9-5; Sun 1-5 (Summer from 10am) Weekend docent tours.
Birds, butterflies, fish, reptiles, mammals, geology and plantlife featured in displays that are an education and pleasure to all ages. Colorful Indian dress and artifacts, with an exhibit tracing local Indian life through the ages. **Planetarium**:- Shows on Sunday afternoons and evenings; Children 50¢; Adults $1. Additional shows through the year. Observatory open Sunday evenings, weather permitting, for telescope viewing.

Historical Society Museum   **Admission Free**
136 E. De la Guerra; 966-1601
Tues-Fri noon-5pm; Sat-Sun 1-5pm; Closed Mondays
Historical memorabilia from Santa Barbara's colorful past. Spanish tiaras, shawls, fans and costumes worn in weddings and gay fandangos during Spanish and Mexican periods. Elaborate, hand-carved Chinese shrine from Santa Barbara's vanished China-town.

Carriage Museum   **Admission Free**
129 Castillo St., 962-2353
Sun 2-5pm (May-Sept); Daily 10-4 (June-Aug.)
Collection of carriages, wagons, stagecoaches, and a horse-drawn fire truck from days before the 'horseless carriage'. Many are brought out to ride in the annual Fiesta Parade.

Entrance to the former Guard's House of the Spanish Presidio, El Cuartel (left). Above is a tiled rooftop within the Santa Barbara Mission grounds.

HISTORIC BUILDINGS

Santa Barbara's bygone eras are reflected in many structures along her streets. The Santa Barbara Mission is the most famous of Santa Barbara's historic buildings, though it is not the oldest. El Cuartel and La Caneda Adobe (private residence), which were part of the Spanish Presidio, are among the oldest remaining buildings.

A drive along Garden Street into hills of the Riviera and beyond to the lovely homes and estates of Montecito reveals a wealth of architecture from the past and the present. The following structures are open to the public for a glimpse of Santa Barbara life in days gone by:

Mission Santa Barbara (founded 1786), Upper Laguna St. Open Mon-Sat 9am-4:45pm; Sun 1-4:45pm.
The well-known "Queen of the Missions," tenth of 21 Franciscan missions in California, is discussed on pages 12-14.
El Cuartel (1782), 122 E. Canon Perdido St. Open Mon-Fri 10:30am-noon & 1-4pm.
The guard's house in El Presidio of Santa Barbara. See pg. 11 for its location within the Presidio.
Fernald House, 414 W. Montecito. Open Sunday only.
A 14-room, multi-gabled Victorian home, richly furnished in the style of the age.
Trussel-Winchester Adobe (1854), 414 W. Montecito St. Open Sunday only.
Sharing the grounds of Fernald House is the adobe home of a seafarer who used timbers from a shipwreck to brace his structure.
Stowe House (1872), 304 Los Carneros Rd., Goleta. (3 blks N. from Los Carneros exit on Hwy. 101) Open Sat-Sun 2-4 pm.
Gingerbread detailing and a sweeping veranda are part of the facade of this gracious country home built in 1872. A carriage house and a bunkhouse containing a collection of Chumash artifacts are on the park-like garden grounds. The house is furnished with an interesting collection of period antiques.

NATURE

Birds

Bird habitats are numerous in the Santa Barbara area, accomodating diverse species ranging from shore-birds to desert fowl. Annual species counts generally reach above 200 with Santa Barbara leading the nation in one recent count.

The California Condor, largest of North American land birds and a master of flight, is a rare and reportedly spectacular sight as it soars above the Santa Barbara backcountry. In its two mountain sanctuaries, Sisquoc in Santa Barbara County and Sespe Wildlife Area in nearby Ventura County, the last of the California Condors may number as few as 30 to 40 adults. Roosting in caves along rugged cliffs, the condor lays only one egg in two years, contributing (along with hunters and en-croaching civilization) to its dimishing population. In gold rush days their quills were used as containers for gold dust. Those fortunate enough to glimpse the condor will recognize the adult by its vast 9-foot wingspan, white triangular patches under each wing and a feather-less orange head and neck.

The Santa Barbara chapter of the Audubon Society offers frequent bird outings, also providing Dial-A-Bird (964-8240) for bird watchers to learn about up-to-date sightings in the area. Of particular interest to birdwatchers are the Botanical Gardens, the Harbor and the Goleta Slough. The Museum of Natural History may be contacted for further suggestions and information.

Butterflies

In February of each year Monarch butterflies gather in selected cypress, eucalyptus and pine groves of Santa Barbara. Their dense clusters are a striking sight as they hang with their wings down for protection from the wind and cold. The clustering is thought to benefit the mating process. They often congregate in the follow-ing areas: Music Academy of the West, More Mesa, Hope Ranch, Butterfly Lane, El Capitan and Gaviota. By mid-March the large gatherings have dispersed.

Among the largest of butterflies in the area with a three to four inch wingspan, the Monarch is recognized by its bright orange wings with black veins. It might be confused, however, with its imitator, the Viceroy. Since the Monarch's diet of milkweed makes it unpalatable to predators, imitation of the Monarch's patterning is is protective to the smaller butterfly.

Tidepools

Hermit crabs, starfish, anemones and sea urchins are among the residents likely to be discovered in their tidepool homes. Coal Oil Point at Devereux Beach, Arroyo Burro, Santa Barbara Point at Leadbetter Beach and Goleta Point are good areas for searching the tidepools. Tide tables are found on the weather page of the newspaper and low tide is the best time for exploring.

Channel Islands

The Channel Islands, "California's Galapagos," harbor rich plant and animal life little touched by 20th century civilization. Dwarf foxes and spotted skunks have developed in their island isolation. Pelicans share the sun-baked rocks with seals and sea lions. Other inhabitants of the different islands include wild boar, elk and snow deer, mule deer, sheep and cattle. The relics of ancient Indian cultures are also woven into the fabric of the islands. A painted Chumash cave on Santa Cruz Island may be reached by sailing or rowing into the cavern.

Transportation to the islands is limited to private craft, day trips and self-sustained overnight camping trips to windswept Anacapa Island from Ventura (call Island Packers, 1-642-1393 for reservations) and field trips to Santa Rosa Island sponsored by the Santa Barbara Museum of Natural History. Those travelling in private crafts require permission to land on the islands. The Channel Islands Monument in Ventura (1-644-8157) has helpful information on visiting the islands.

Whales

The California Grey Whale migrates north each spring from the warm waters off Baja California to summer feeding grounds in the Bering Sea. February through April whale watchers may spy the white-spotted mammoth spouting from kelpbeds along the Santa Barbara coast. This great sea mammal grows 40-50 feet in length, its tail fin alone weighing as much as 400 lbs.

Shoreline Park provides a good vantage for whale watchers. SEA Landing at the Harbor (963-3564) offers seasonal cruises that may afford a closer look at the majestic denizen of the sea. Contact the Museum of Natural History for more information about the California Grey Whale.

Stalking the Grunion

Flashlights flicker along moonlit shores. Ocean rhythms and murmuring voices are suddenly split by frantic splashing and jubilant yelps — and the grunion hunt is on!

Indians used to say that fish dance on the beaches during a full moon. They were likely referring to a spawning "dance" that grunion perform after riding ashore on the highest waves of summer. A female buries herself tail-first in the sand where she deposits her eggs. Gyrating about her, the male fertilizes the eggs as they are laid. Young, newly-hatched grunion are washed out to sea in the next high tide.

Enthusiastic grunion hunters grab at the first sound of flapping fish in the sand. Naturally, however, it is best to await spawning when taking part in the bare-handed stalk of the wriggling moonlight dancers.

HIKING

Miles of trails wind through the hills and canyons in and around Santa Barbara. A good place to begin hiking is in the Botanical Gardens (1½ miles N. of the Mission on Mission Canyon Rd.) where easy trails meander through wildflower meadows, woodlands and chaparral.

The local chapter of the Sierra Club leads frequent group hikes designed for varied hiking abilities. The Sierra Club's Friday evening hike, which meets at the Mission parking lot at 6:15 p.m. (bring a flashlight), is an easy to moderate hike suitable for beginners — and everyone is welcome. For information about other Sierra Club activities, call 962-2210.

The following are four popular nearby trails:

JESUSITA TRAIL

Grade: Moderate
Starting Elevation: 400 ft.
Final Elevation: 250 ft.
Elevation Gain: 850 ft.
Distance: 2 miles to Inspiration Point; another mile to intersection with Tunnel Trail.
Trail Begins: Either 1) north end of Stevens Park, or, 2) just north of Cater Water Filtration Plant (San Roque Rd., north of Foothill Rd.)

RATTLESNAKE TRAIL

Grade: Moderate
Starting Elevation: 1100 ft.
Final Elevation: 2000 ft.
Elevation Gain: 900 ft.
Distance: 1½ mi. to Tin Can Junction; trail branches west to meet Tunnel Trail & east to Gibraltar Rd. (either fork approx. ½ mi.+500 ft.)
Trail Begins: West of the stone bridge that crosses creek (Las Canoas Rd.).
Note: Carrying drinking water is advised.

TUNNEL TRAIL

Grade: Moderate at lower levels; difficult on upper trail
Starting Elevation: 1250 ft.
Final Elevation: 3500 ft.
Elevation Gain: 2250 ft.
Distance: 4-5 miles to E. Camino Cielo; west on Camino Cielo is La Cumbre Peak Lookout.
Trail Begins: Along Old Road, just beyond locked gate at north end of Tunnel Rd.
Note: Hikers should carry water and prepare for full sun (almost no shade along trail).

COLD SPRINGS TRAIL

Grade: Moderate hiking around pools at lower level; steep grade and difficult hike to upper level.
Starting Elevation: 750 ft.
Final Elevation: 3250 ft.
Elevation Gain: 2500 ft.
Distance: 3¼ miles to E. Camino Cielo.
Trail Begins: 4/10 mi. east of intersection of Cold Springs Rd. and Mountain Drive.
Note: Creek is filled most of the year and has lovely pools both on and off the trail at the lower level.

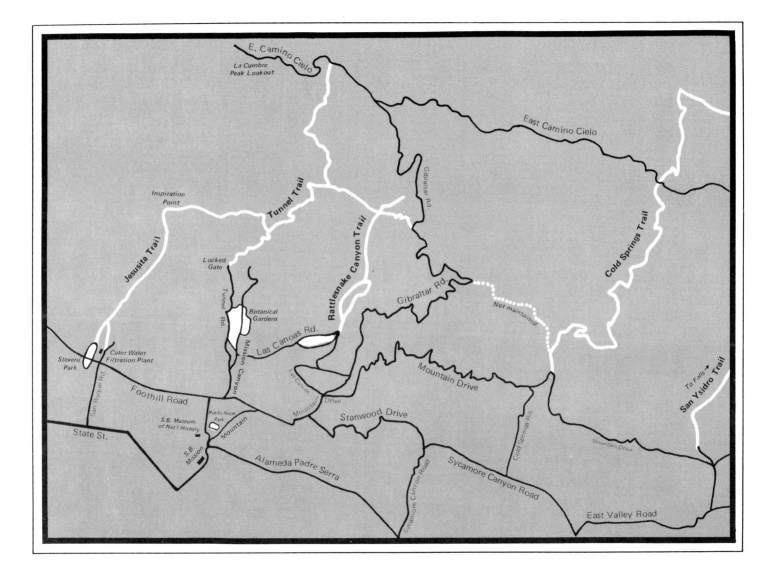

EDUCATION

Educational institutions offering instruction in the arts, academics and/or vocational skills number over two dozen in the Santa Barbara area, including:

University of California at Santa Barbara

10 miles west of Santa Barbara, Ward Memorial Blvd. exit from Hwy. 101 (adjacent to Santa Barbara Airport); Mailing address: UCSB, Santa Barbara, CA 93106; Information (805) 961-2311

UCSB annually enrolls approx. 14,000 students in over 80 fields of study at its scenic coastal campus. Music and dance concerts, films, exhibits, sporting events and dramatic productions at the University are generally open to the public. UCSB is one of nine campuses in the highly regarded University of California educational system.

Santa Barbara City College

721 Cliff Drive, Santa Barbara CA 93109; 965-0581

A two-year community college, SBCC draws over 8,000 students each year to its cliff-top campus overlooking the harbor. Free admission is available to residents (one year California residency & local address by registration) pursuing any of SBCC's varied courses of study.

Westmont College

955 La Paz Rd. Santa Barbara, CA 93108; 969-5051

Westmont is an independent non-denominational Christian college of liberal arts. Its lovely residential campus is set in the hills of Montecito.

SBCC Adult Education

914 Santa Barbara St.; 962-8144

One of the finest continuing education programs in the country is centered at a pleasant mid-town campus in Santa Barbara. Dozens of rich and varied courses, taught by highly qualified instructors, stimulate the thoughts, skills and creativity of Santa Barbara's continuing students.

Brooks Institute of Photography

2190 Alston Rd., Santa Barbara, CA 93108; 2020 Alameda Padre Serra; 1321 Alameda Padre Serra; 969-2291

Spectacular city and ocean views spread before each of the hillside campuses of the well-known school of photography. Bachelor of Arts degrees are offered in photography. Free guided tours scheduled. Photo Gallery, 2020 Alameda Padre Serra; Hall of Fame, 1321 Alameda Padre Serra.

Music Academy of the West

1070 Fairway Road, Santa Barbara 93108; 969-4726

Summer music program for gifted students offers the opportunity to study with masters. Students perform for the public in the Music Academy's popular summer concert series.

SHOPPING

Downtown

Santa Barbara's downtown shopping area is an attractively landscaped string of shops extending primarily from Ortega to Victoria Streets along State and adjoining streets.

El Paseo
800 block east of State St.
A picturesque maze of stone pathways meander through white stucco shops, a patio cafe and open-roofed restaurant. Developed around historic Casa de la Guerra, El Paseo is entered by a pathway opposite De la Guerra Plaza called "A Street in Spain". Other paths enter from State and Anacapa Streets.

Paseo San Marcos
1100 block west of State St.
Site of a popular garden restaurant.

La Arcada Court
1000 block east of State St.
Patio restaurant in attractive shopping court.

Victoria Court
1200 block west of State St.
A new paseo of shops.

Picadilly Square
813 State St.
A flourishing arcade of vendors in an open-walled, bi-level marketplace across from El Paseo.

Brinkerhoff Avenue
2½ blocks west of State St. between Cota & Haley Sts.
Quaint Victorian houses line the single block street under a row of stately palms. All along the street, old-fashioned houses have been turned into antique and curio shops.

Beach

Sunday Art Show-on-the-Boulevard
East of State St. along Cabrillo Blvd.
For over half a mile, local artists display their handiwork under the palms. Paintings, batiks, wood and leather crafts, hand-made clothing, jewelry and pottery are among the colorful array each Sunday from 10 a.m. to sunset.

Uptown

La Cumbre Plaza
3800 block of upper State St. at La Cumbre Rd.
Shopping mall with Mediterranean architectural styling and open-air walkways between shops.

Montecito

Two attractive shopping areas cater to well-to-do residents of the lovely village community: Coast Village Rd. (101 south to Hot Springs Rd. exit) and East Valley Rd. either side of San Ysidro Road (take Olive Mill Rd. north to E. Valley Road and head east ½ mile).

Solvang and Ojai

Two communities within easy driving distance of Santa Barbara have interesting shops in attractive settings. Danish Solvang abounds with European import shops, bakeries and restaurants with Old World charm.

Popular with shoppers
on Sundays is the
art and craft show
under the palms
at the beach.

SURROUNDINGS

At Santa Barbara's doorstep are places well-worth exploring.

Montecito

In a valley and wooded hills that once swarmed with grizzly bear (and sold for just pennies an acre) are the fabulous estates and lovely homes of Montecito.

A favorite hideaway for bandits and other social misfits during Mexican times, the Montecito valley was first settled by retiring Spanish soldiers granted land for their years of service. The Montecito Hot Springs, used for centuries by Indians and Spanish-speaking residents for bathing and medicinal purposes, became widely acclaimed in the 1870's and drew flocks of wealthy Easterners. Many returned to build the first of Montecito's grand estates. The springs are now part of the village's water system.

A drive through Montecito, past attractive shopping areas (see SHOPPING) to winding residential lanes, may offer glimpses of romantic estates and gardens beyond sheltering groves of oak and sycamore.

Ojai

East of Montecito and inland along route 150 is the beautiful Ojai Valley (pronounced OH-hi). Visitors may view the lush valley seen as "Shangri-La" in the famous film "Lost Horizons" (east on Ojai Ave. to the viewing bench near the hilltop). The Taj Mahal of India has a look-alike on Avenida de la Vereda. Many visitors to the Ojai Valley enjoy the relaxing mineral waters in the bath house of Matilija Hot Springs (788 W. Hot Springs Rd., 646-7667). World-famous potter Beatrice Wood has opened her show place studios to the public (8560 Hwy. 150, 646-3381).

Lake Casitas nearby offers nearly 100 miles of fresh water shoreline with hidden coves and inlets. Bass, trout, crappie and catfish challenge fishermen. Ashore there are boat and motor rentals, bait, sailboats, riding stables, snack bar and hundreds of camping spaces for tents and trailers.

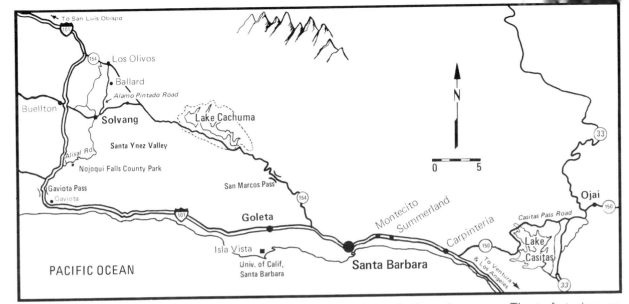

Solvang and the San Ynez Valley

Across San Marcos Pass in the heart of the San Ynez Valley is the tiny Danish community of Solvang. Like "a page from Hans Christian Andersen," Solvang is a town of cobblestone walks, thatched roofs, gas streetlights and windmills turning in the breeze. Storks stand on rooftops as bearers of good luck. Aromas of pastries, chocolate and Old World cuisine draw guests to the many bakeries and restaurants where preparation often follows Danish traditions.

"Sunny valley," as Solvang translates, was selected in the early 1900's to be the site for a Danish-American community. Thousands celebrate the town's heritage each September in Solvang's Danish Days festival.

Theater-goers flock to the summer **Theaterfest** where an excellent repertory company performs in Solvang's open-air Festival Theater. Mission Santa Ines contrasts with its Danish surroundings, one of the best preserved of the Spanish missions.

Solvang may be reached via Hwy. 101 and east through Buellton, though Hwy. 154 offers a more scenic route. That drive passes the **Lake Cachuma** recreation area, a popular site for camping, fishing, sailing, boating, hiking and horse riding at the largest man-made fresh water lake in Southern California. Historic stagecoach stop Mattei's Tavern is farther along in Los Olivos and in Ballard there is a one-room schoolhouse still in use since its opening in 1883.

Windmill in Solvang.

DINING

Call for times and reservations.

Continental

La Grange 1327 State St., 962-5607
Excellent French cuisine prepared with skill and care by French owner-chef.

Chanticleer 1279 Coast Village Rd. (Montecito), 969-5959
Elegant dining. Cocktails & fine wine list.

Casa de Sevilla 428 Chapala St. 966-4370 (Closed Sun/Mon)
Seafood, steaks and Spanish dishes at restaurant serving Santa Barbara over half a century. Dress code.

Talk of the Town 123 W. Gutierrez St. 966-4910
Extensive menu, open fireplace, cocktails, strict dress code.

Dinner Houses

Eleven-29 1129 State St., 963-7704
Attractive restaurant with a garden-like setting. Cocktails. Luncheons and patio service. Nightly entertainment.

Olive Mill Bistro 1295 Coast Village Rd. (Montecito) 969-4900. Longtime Santa Barbara dinner and night spot. Cocktails, piano bar & dancing.

Teasers 1533 State St. 966-4263
Large and varied menu from burgers to full course meals. Cocktails & entertainment.

Cafe del Sol 516 San Ysidro Rd. (Montecito) 969-9448
Relaxed setting with Mexican & Spanish dishes, seafood & Steaks. Patio luncheons, cocktails, entertainment.

Cold Spring Tavern 5995 Stagecoach Rd. (20 min. from town off 154) 967-0066. Rustic tavern and dinner house thought to be a former stagecoach stop. Entertainment.

Hotel Restaurants

Santa Barbara Biltmore 1260 Channel Dr. (Montecito) 969-2261. Beautiful ocean setting and Mediterranean architecture. Cocktails, entertainment, Sunday champagne brunch and Sunday evening buffet.

Mar Monte Hotel & Spa 1111 E. Cabrillo Blvd. 963-0744
Attractive oceanfront restaurant. Cocktails, entertainment and three dance floors.

Don the Beachcomber 435 S. Milpas (at the beach on Cabrillo) Santa Barbara Inn, 966-2285. Polynesian decor and cuisine. Ocean views, cocktails, entertainment and dancing.

San Ysidro Ranch 900 San Ysidro Lane (Montecito) 969-5046. Breakfast, lunch, dinner served at historic guest ranch. (Ranch guests have included an interesting parade of film personalities and world leaders.)

International

El Paseo 813 Anacapa St. 965-5106
Open-air dining in the heart of El Paseo. Spanish Colonial decor and Mexican specialties. Cocktails and fireplace.

Espana 29 E. Cabrillo Blvd. 963-1968
Waterfront restaurant serving Spanish-American dishes, seafoods & steaks. Cocktails and entertainment.

Tiny's Mexican Restaurant 2251 Las Positas, 682-5454
Attractive Mexican restaurant across Hwy. 101 from the Earl Warren Showgrounds.

Nacho's 2829 De la Vina, 687-3014
Mexican meals served in a cozy atmosphere.

Mom's Italian Village 421 E. Cota St. 965-5588
Italian specialties served in comfortable Old World surroundings.

With over 250 dining establishments in the area, it has been said that Santa Barbara has more restaurants per capita than any place south of San Francisco. Quaint and interesting restaurants may be discovered in shopping paseos along State Street, along the waterfront, in lovely Monetecito, or off the beaten paths. A few of the many popular area restaurants have been selected to give newcomers a starting place for discovering their own favorites.

The Plaka 235 W. Montecito St. 965-9622
Folk and belly dancing are often part of the floor show highlighted by the proprietor's amazing table dance (he dances with a dinner table in his teeth — honestly!). Greek dinner specialties. Cocktails.

Cafe Suisse 133 N. Fairview Ave. (In Fairview Center, Goleta) 964-2747. Small restaurant with veal specialties.

Jimmy's Oriental Gardens 126 E. Canon Perdido St. 962-7582. Cantonese and American selections in popular downtown location.

Mandarin Cuisine 3514 State St. 682-2606
A nice combination is their wonton soup, egg roll and moo goo guy pan.

Cherry Blossom 3026 State St. 682-2210
Japanese cuisine, wines, beer and sake.

Tokyo Inn 2710 De la Vina, 687-0210
Japanese cuisine, private tatami rooms, sushi bar.

Van's Belgian Waffles 922 State St. 962-0808
Crepes and thick Belgian waffles.

Seafood & Steaks

Chuck's Steak House 3888 State St. 687-4417
Steaks and seafood. Teriyaki steak specialty. Cocktails.

Chart House 101 E. Cabrillo Blvd. 966-2112
Oceanfront restaurant serving steaks & seafood.

Pelican's Wharf 1212 Coast Vlg. Rd. (Montecito) 969-2243
Seafood, prime ribs and steaks.

Lobster House 15 E. Cabrillo Blvd. 965-1174
Reasonably-priced seafood specialties served cafeteria-style overlooking the beach. Select fish from fresh catch list.

Family Dining

The Big Yellow House 108 Pierpont Ave. (Summerland) 969-4414. Family-oriented dining in handsomely remodeled restaurant dating from the turn of the century.

J.K. Frimples, 1701 State St. 962-3671
Built around an enormous fig tree that once had wallabies sharing its glassed enclosure. Outdoor patio. Open 24 hrs.

Casual Fare

Eggception Omelet & Deli House 1208 State St. 965-7942
Over 100 omelets served in a friendly atmosphere.

Epicurean Catering Company 125 E. Carrillo St. 966-4789
Interesting luncheon fare served in an attractive garden setting. Dinner served Friday & Saturday by reservation.

Sojourner Coffee House 134 E. Canon Perdido 965-7922
Vegetarian soups and sandwiches (some non-vegetarian selections), homemade desserts and fine coffees.

Earthling Book & Tea Room 22 E. Victoria St. 962-6936
Afternoon teas or fruit beverages served with sandwiches and home-baked pastries.

The Farmer and the Fisherman Hwy. 101 N. to Gaviota 685-2657. Restaurant and stores with natural foods, many of which are from the Sunburst Community Farms. (See INLAND for information on touring the farms.)

The Good Earth 21 W. Canon Perdido St. 962-4463
Sandwiches and natural food specialties.

The Elegant Farmer 5555 Hollister Ave. (Goleta) 967-3200
Attractive restaurant with outdoor patio, luncheon and dinner menus. For lunch try the "Omaha" and walnut pie.

Flapper Alley 5112 Hollister Ave. 964-8656
Pizza, burgers, salads & sandwiches served in attractive surroundings. Cocktails.

ALSO...

Entertainment

Arlington Center for the Performing Arts 1317 State St. 966-9382. Dance, rock & symphony concerts, stage productions and films.

Lobero Theatre 33 E. Canon Perdido, 963-0761 Plays, concerts and lectures throughout the year.

Santa Barbara County Bowl 1122 N. Milpas 963-8634 Rock concerts and other productions in the beautiful outdoor ampitheatre.

Earl Warren Showgrounds Hwy 101 at Las Positas 687-0766. A continuing program of events including horse shows, carnivals, flower shows, rodeos and the circus. See ANNUAL EVENTS and call for further information.

University of California, Santa Barbara Concerts, films, lectures, dance and theatrical performances are part of the continuing program of University events. Call UCSB Arts & Lectures (961-3535) for events schedule.

Solvang Theaterfest 420 2nd, Solvang 688-7688 Fine summer repertory performances in open-air theater. Take warm wraps for the performances.

Music Academy of the West 1070 Fairway Rd. (Montecito) 969-4726. Popular summer concert series.

For information on night spots and current offerings in the area, consult the Saturday "Liesure Section" of the *Santa Barbara News-Press* or the calendar section of the weekly alternative paper, the *Santa Barbara News & Review. This Week in Santa Barbara* has further listings.

Hotels & Motels

A listing of hotels and motels is available from the Santa Barbara Chamber of Commerce. 1301 Santa Barbara St., Santa Barbara, CA 93101, 965-3021.

Camping

City Parks: Tent camping in Skofield Park (See PARKS).
County Parks: Cachuma Lake, 21 mi NW of SB via Hwy. 154 (805) 688-4658.
State Parks: One week limit 6/1-9/30; 30 day limit 10/1-5/31; Reservations accepted 7-90 days in advance for site fee plus $1 to Dept. of Parks & Rec., P.O. Box 2390, Sacramento, CA 95811 or through Ticketron outlets. Carpinteria Beach Park, 12 mi. SE of SB via Hwy. 101, $4 campsites, $5 trailers.
El Capitan Beach, 18 mi. W of SB via Hwy. 101, $4 & $5 campsites.
Refugio Beach, 19 mi. W of SB via Hwy. 101 (no reservations - first come basis.)
Los Padres National Forest: Contact the Forest Service, 42 Aero Camino, Goleta, CA 93017, (805) 963-3611 for information about camping in the National Forest.

For Further Information

The Santa Barbara Chamber of Commerce has printed matter available on a number of topics of visitor and resident interest, most free of charge. Publications topics include: accomodations, restaurants, night spots, campsites, fishing and street maps (35¢). Call or write the Chamber at 1301 Santa Barbara St., Santa Barbara, CA 93101, (805) 965-3021.

Index

Book design & layout by author

Santa Barbara Highlights Map by Marin Graphics
Printing by Bellwood
Roeder-Shipley Printing Brokers

Photo Credits:

Cover Photo: Steven R. Nelson

Color Photography:
Inside color photography by James Neihouse except:
Harbor Sails, Leon Bonotaux
Chumash Canoe, Peter Howorth
Sandcastle, Lucinda Houtchens

Black/White Photography:
Chumash woodcutter, S.B. Hist. Soc. Collection
Earthquake photos, Courtesy UCSB Special Collections
Fiesta dancer (Rosal Ortega), Leon Bonotaux
Seal, James Neihouse
UCSB Aerial View, United Aerial Survey, Courtesy
   UCSB Special Collections
The following photos courtesy Santa Barbara Chamber of Commerce:
Mother & child (6), Mural Room (25), Boat Rentals (32), Golfers (34),
Hikers (44), Art fair (49), Solvang (50), Restaurant (52).

All other photography by author.
Many B/W photos custom finished by Randle Photo Labs.